Butterfly Kisses
and
Wishes on Wings

When someone you love has cancer
… a hopeful, helpful book for kids

Written by Ellen McVicker

Illustrated by Nanci Hersh

Butterfly Kisses and Wishes on Wings is a gem. This is a very important book with a very powerful message. A beautiful work of art that educates children about medical and psychological issues relating to cancer, it is also a gift for the loved one with cancer. As the public television personality Doc Neil the Banana Peel, I have had the opportunity to perform for kids and adults with cancer to help them relax and enjoy life. For a patient with cancer, there is no better gift than the comforting words and hugs from a kid who understands … it brightens the day. ***Butterfly Kisses and Wishes on Wings*** provides a pathway to this gift.

Neil Shulman, MD, author of *What's in a Doctor's Bag?*
Associate professor, Emory University School of Medicine
Author and associate producer, "Doc Hollywood" starring Michael J. Fox
President, Patch Adams' Gesundheit! Institute

www.butterflykissesbook.com

Dedication

Nanci and her boys - 2002

Nanci and her boys - 2023

This book is lovingly dedicated to my cousin Nanci Hersh's sons, Griffin and Nate who, when ages 5 and 3, put on *their* butterfly wings so they too could travel with their mom through her cancer journey.

And in loving memory of a remarkable visionary...

Dr. Beth Deutch, 1960-2014

Founder of HerSpace Breast Imaging Associates, Monmouth County, NJ.
Dr. Deutch was an award-winning radiologist and visionary women's health advocate, Nanci's doctor, and ultimately- her friend. Dr. Deutch was brilliant, accomplished, compassionate, and passionate about supporting women, loved the arts, and above all- her husband Larry, and their three children.

Foreword

"How will I explain this to my children?" has impressively been the frequent first response of my young patients receiving the diagnosis of breast cancer. This speaks to how we love the children in our lives and place their well-being in front of our own. It also speaks to a need we all have in explaining cancer and illness to young children and helping them, when necessary, to be an integral part of the journey. We now recognize that to do otherwise is unhealthy. This was Nanci's concern when I delivered the news of breast cancer to her in 2002. The narrative in **Butterfly Kisses and Wishes on Wings** was her loving cousin Ellen's gift to her and her young sons. Through Nanci's beautiful and poignant illustrations, and the collaboration between cousins – the special education/kindergarten school teacher and the artist/breast cancer survivor – the gift is now for us all to cherish and use.

When Nanci first showed me this book, I cried. I cried as a mother of young children, for the clarity it brings to the young child's mind by answering the questions that he may not yet be able to formulate and by calming the fears that he may not yet recognize. I cried as a breast imager who daily delivers the news of breast cancer – that mothers and fathers will have one less source of anxiety with this book as a resource.

When you fly alongside the butterfly through the pages of this book, I have no doubt that you, too, will appreciate its value. It is not just for the child in the midst of a family illness. It is for all children and all parents everywhere.

-Dr. Beth Deutch, Medical Director of **HerSpace**: Breast Imaging Associates

Dear Readers,

The text of ***Butterfly Kisses* and *Wishes on Wings*** was originally written as a gift for my cousin Nanci Hersh, an award-winning artist, to help her find the right words to explain her cancer diagnosis to her then 3–year-old and 5–year-old boys. Two years later, and finally in remission - along with some gentle nudging on my part, Nanci agreed to illustrate the text I had written for her boys.

Once our endeavor was completed, we realized that ***Butterfly Kisses and Wishes on Wings*** had become much more than a simple story. Through clear, candid text, and Nanci's exquisite illustrations, it had evolved into a resource that could be used to educate and support many other children around the world who are facing the cancer of a loved one.

We are pleased that you have chosen our book to help guide you as you teach a child about cancer. We hope our words and pictures will foster an honest and open dialogue between you and the child listening or reading along. Additionally, we hope that you will see the magic that ***Butterfly Kisses and Wishes on Wings*** has in bringing children to a clearer understanding of cancer, and the realization that they have great power within themselves to be an active and integral part of their loved one's cancer journey.

With butterfly wishes,
Ellen McVicker

P.S. We offer many wonderful resources for children and their families on our website. Please visit us at **www.butterflykissesbook.com**, or contact the author directly at (303) 589 -2099

*A butterfly kiss is a fluttering of one's eyelashes on someone's cheek …which often makes them smile and giggle.

The other day my mom
went to the doctor.

She didn't even look sick,
but she said she had to go anyway.

I remember when she came home ...

she looked worried and sad.

Later, my mom said she needed to
tell me something really important.

She wanted to tell me why she went to see the doctor.

But, when she started to tell me,

she looked worried and sad all over again.

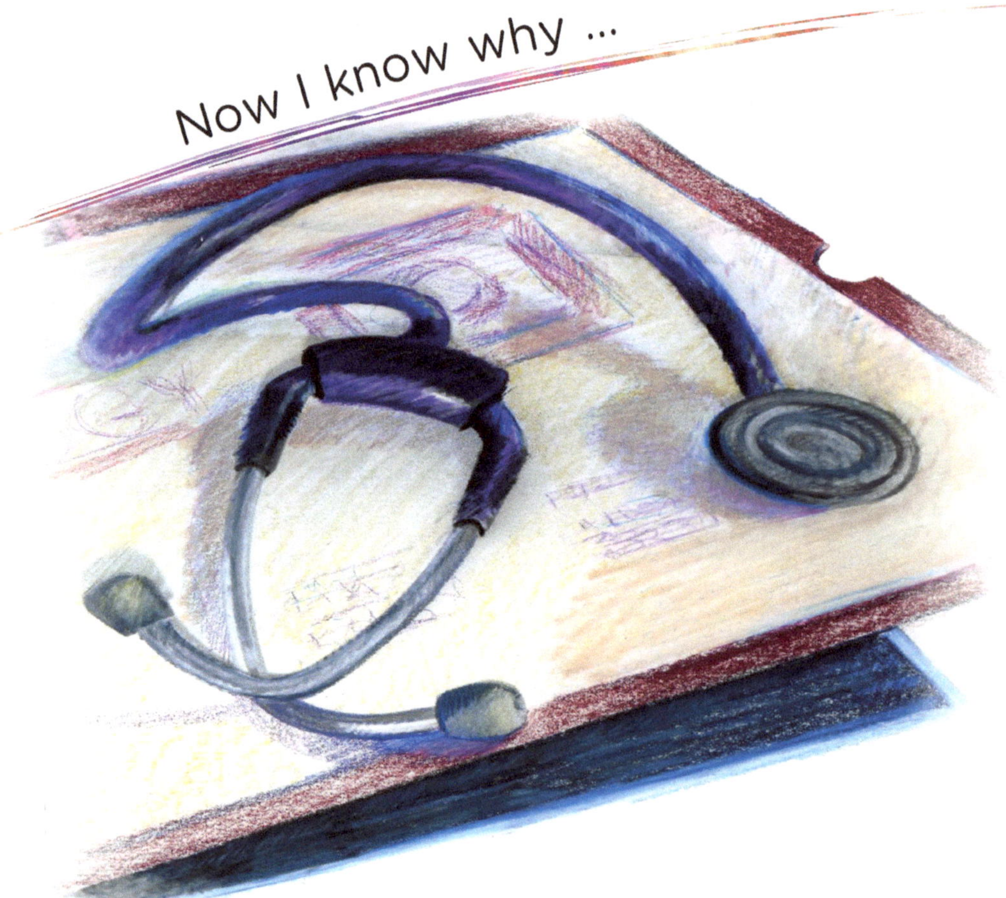
Now I know why ...

The doctor told my mom she has cancer.

I wasn't sure what cancer was, so I asked my mom,

"What is cancer?"

She said it isn't like a cold or a cough or
even the flu.
She said it's hard to explain.

I asked her to try anyway.

Mom said that everyone's body is made up of millions and billions of tiny cells —

so tiny, you need a microscope to see them.

Cancer happens when some of the good cells in your body change to bad cells. No one knows why they change. They just do. It's kind of like they get sick.

Before you know it, more and more of the bad cancer cells are in your body AND they're stopping the GOOD cells from doing the job they're supposed to do.

Doctors who know all about this stuff can help people get rid of the bad cancer cells ...

and there are lots of different ways they can do it.

Some people may go to the hospital for an operation, where the doctor tries to take out all the cancer cells.

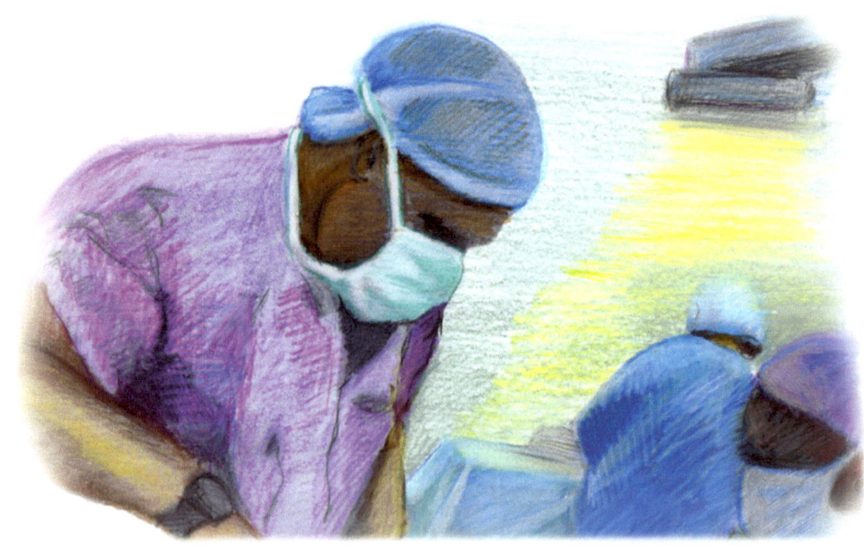

Some people may need something called radiation. Mom said that radiation is this beam of light that the doctor uses to kill the bad cancer cells.

It's kind of like my toy laser sword.

And some people may need
a special kind of medicine
called chemotherapy ...
but, most people just call it "chemo."

Mom said if she has to have the chemo, it
could make her tired or give her tummy
aches. It may even make her hair fall out!
That means she would be bald, but probably
not forever. Her hair could grow back when
she starts to get better.

I don't even care if
my mom does get bald.
The medicine would destroy
the cancer cells,
and that's JUST what we want!

We're not sure what
my mom needs yet.

She said the doctor will
help her decide.

My mom has cancer.
Oh, no! I wonder ...

Did I do anything to make her get cancer?

If I hug and kiss my mom, will I get cancer, too?

When I asked my mom, she smiled and said I didn't
do anything to make her get sick,
and that cancer is NOT contagious.

That means I can't catch cancer from her
or anyone else.

She even gave me a pinkie promise.

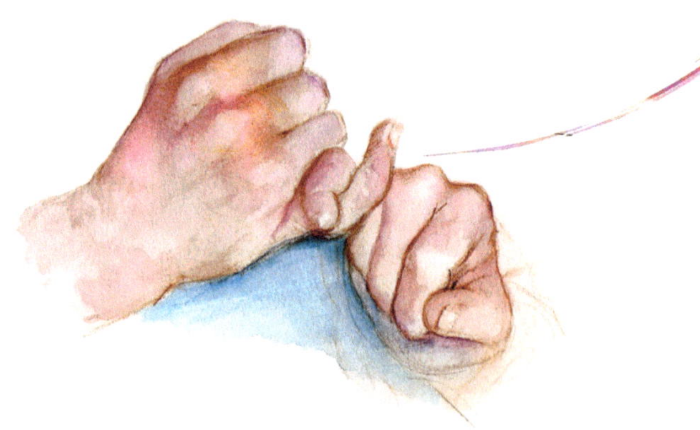

So ...

I can still take bites of her peanut butter and jelly sandwich and have a sip of her juice.

We can even share an ice cream cone. Strawberry is our favorite!

And when we cross the street, Mom can hold my hand ... just like always.

Best of all,

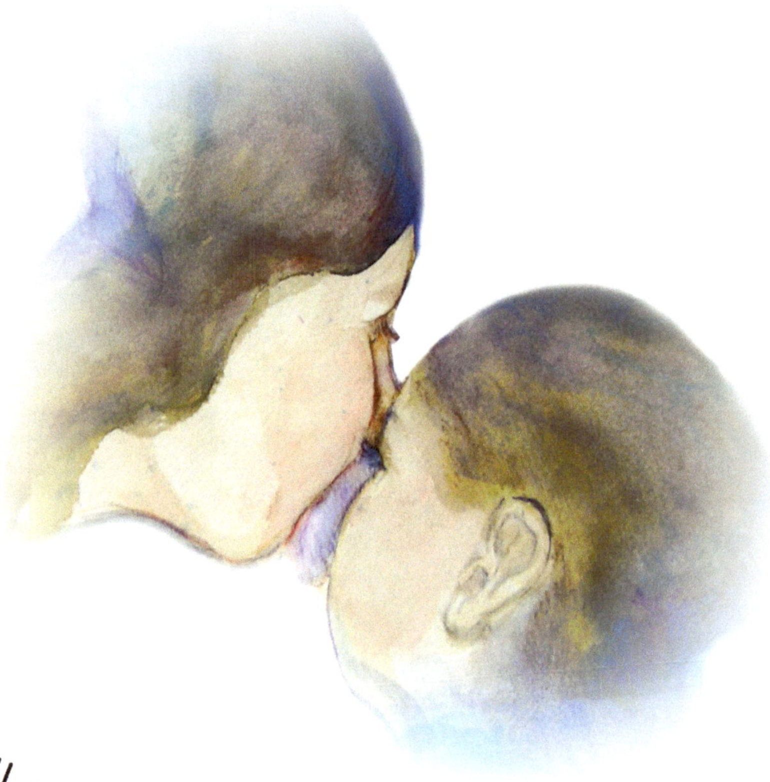

we can still cuddle and give lots of kisses —

butterfly kisses ... Eskimo kisses

... kisses on our cheeks.

No matter what we do together, or how many
kisses we give each other,
I WON'T catch her cancer.

Mom said the doctor will do everything she can to help her get better.

I can't make her cancer go away,
but I can do lots of other things!

I can bring her a tissue,

or get her a glass of water
... even if I spill a little.

When she's resting,
I can cover her toes
with a blanket
so she doesn't
get chilly.

I can feed Maizie, our cat, and even brush her.

I can brush my own hair, too.
Mom laughs, because sometimes
I just use the same brush.

And getting dressed all by myself won't be so hard ...

So what if my clothes don't match!

If Mom needs a nap,

I'll play with my little brother so he doesn't wake her up. He can be so noisy!

But, before
she takes
her nap,

I'll read her one of our favorite books.

If Grandma or Auntie calls and asks me to spend the night,

If Grandma or Auntie calls and asks me to spend the night,

Mom says I should go.

It would give me a break ...

and everyone needs a break now and then.

I'll even draw my mom a picture every day.

My pictures always
make her smile,

and right now Mom
needs a bunch
of smiles!

Mom really loves it
when I draw her
butterflies!

She says they remind her of our butterfly kisses,

and big hugs and kisses are
what she needs most —

especially my butterfly kisses!

*My mom once told me that the wings of a butterfly are magical.
If you watch a butterfly as it flutters its wings through the air,
the butterfly will bring you good luck.*

Now, more than ever, I need to be my mom's butterfly!

Mom also told me I might have lots of different feelings inside me.

She says some kids get SAD and feel LONELY when
someone they love has cancer.

Some kids get MAD.

And then there are kids who WORRY a lot.

I'm already worried.

I worry and wonder if Mom
    will ever be okay again.

I HATE that my mom has cancer!
It SCARES me.
Mom says it scares her, too.

At least we can be scared together.

With all this stuff going on, Mom said it's important
for me to talk about my feelings, and that it's okay to
tell people that she has cancer.

That's good, because talking about things
always makes me feel better inside.

I know I can talk to my dad and my best friend.

Usually I just talk to Maizie.
She's the best listener!

Mom said she also told my teacher

all about her cancer ...

just in case I start thinking about it
when I'm in school.

My mom sure is smart.
She's thought
of everything!

But for now,

I just want to talk to my mom.

I want to give her lots of hugs and butterfly kisses, and tell her that I love her.

# Acknowledgements

There are people who enter our lives and help us realize our potential by guiding us as we travel beyond
what we sometimes believe to be our limits.
We are fortunate to have many of these people in our lives – to them we owe an abundance of thanks.

From Ellen's heart – thank you …

Nanci Hersh, my cousin, whose illustrations inspired the creation of new words and delivered
the message we wanted to share
Cheryl McCallister, an angel who has guided my path professionally and spiritually
Robin Pack and **Rona Goldberg**, my sisters, my friends, and my greatest cheerleaders
Muriel Pizer, my beloved mother, the woman who gave me my butterfly wings and modeled the importance of helping others
Tracey McVicker, my husband, and **Dustin**, **Jordan** and **Chad**, our three boys, who have been my butterflies
always traveling alongside me as I follow my dreams
and, to...
Megan Koltiska and **"Captain" Tom Myers**... in loving memory, thank you both for being the epitome of
living life in the "now" and creating lasting memories with those you loved and all who knew you

From Nanci's heart – thank you …

Ellen McVicker, my cousin, whose gentle persistence in having me illustrate this story
has been a source of support, healing, and love
Dr. Beth Deutch, doctor, art lover, and friend; a butterfly to so many and forever in my heart
Ellen and **Herb Hersh**, my parents whose love gave me the roots and wings to fly
Joy Dight, my mother-in-law, cheerleader and butterfly
Scott Dight, my husband, who comes from love in everything he does – and inspires me to do the same,
and our children, **Griffin** and **Nate Dight**, whose love and laughter always make my heart sing

From both of us ...

Fran Waldmann, a hero in our eyes for designing the book as we dreamed it should be

In loving memory of **Dr. Beth Deutch,** Medical Director of **HerSpace**: Breast Imaging Associates, who believed in our work from the onset

Along with...

You, our readers, for being butterflies to your loved ones who have truly needed you during their cancer journey

and, to...

The many other wonderful, loving, and very courageous people in our lives who have dramatically been affected by cancer. Some have died; some have conquered; some have outcomes yet to be known. Each one has taught us about facing fears, taking charge, and moving on. Those who have passed away taught us about embracing life and dying with dignity.

With respect, gratitude, and our loving hearts - we thank you all.

What Our Readers Have to Say ...

"My own mother died from breast cancer when I was 8 years old. My sister, Lisa, was only five. To this day, I can so vividly remember the confusion I felt, trying to understand why our world was suddenly turned upside down and why no one wanted to talk about it. ... How I wish we had *Butterfly Kisses and Wishes on Wings* - what a gift it would have been! ... This book is precious and full of wonderful messages that are so important and will make such a difference in so many little hearts."

> Maggie O'Brien
> Middletown, New Jersey

"I believe you have captured the innermost feelings of young children. The clarity of reassurance of the child's safety and his/her remaining an integral part of the nuclear family (under the duress of illness) and being able to contribute to the parent's well being resonates in the prose. Simplicity of explanation is necessary in answering difficult questions that children pose to adults, and you have been successful in doing this with your book.

> Shirley MacPherson, Ph.D.
> Clinical Therapist/Psychologist
> Los Angeles, CA

"I read *Butterfly Kisses and Wishes on Wings* with my 6-year-old daughter. She loved the book. Her comment was 'How did the book know what I was thinking?' Your book handled the subject matter with dignity and grace."

> Dr. Sherrie Somers & daughter Chanah
> Denver, Colorado

"Your book really does address extremely well an area that many people forget about during a cancer diagnosis – the impact on the children. They are often the forgotten ones in the crisis. Making children a part of that time is so important – for everyone. I remember I used to use what I called "love therapy." I would hug my boys so tightly that I was convinced it was making me better, because I couldn't possibly imagine not being there for them. Well, it worked."

> Lorry Gaidus, Breast Cancer Survivor (12 years!)
> Upper Saddle River, N.J.

"Did you know that some of the best medicine for some diseases is love and lots of help? I learned that and other things from Mrs. McVicker's book, *Butterfly Kisses and Wishes on Wings*. If anyone wants to read something about cancer, Mrs. McVicker's book is the right way to go."

> Virginia Nystrom
> 3rd grader
> Aurora, CO.

Throughout her professional life, **Ellen McVicker** has always worked in some capacity with children, parents, educators, and people who were dedicated to the mental health profession. As a master teacher in the field of special and regular education, the Director of Education for both Charter Hospital of Denver and the Colorado Children's Museum, and as Marketing Director for the Centre for Behavioral Health at Denver's Porter Memorial Hospital, Ellen would always find ways to fulfill her true life's passion ... **empowering children and their families in challenging situations.**
Today, Ellen McVicker lives in Aurora, Colorado with her husband Tracey. She remains committed to her book ***Butterfly Kisses and Wishes on Wings*** and sharing its many messages with children, families, healthcare professionals, and cancer organizations throughout the world.

Drawing threads from daily life, **Nanci Hersh** is a deep-rooted chronicler of the significant and the mundane, marking time, and holding space to allow for reflection, authentic, and sometimes difficult conversations. Following a diagnosis of breast cancer in 2002 many gifts came Nanci's way, among them were a blank sketchbook from friends, and this story from her cousin Ellen. This was the beginning of a beautiful collaboration, which led Nanci to create the illustrations that have become ***Butterfly Kisses and Wishes on Wings***.

Nanci is also a curator, illustrator, educator, arts advocate, and former Executive Director of the Delaware Institute for the Arts in Education. Nanci lives in beautiful Chester County, Pennsylvania.
You can reach Nanci and see more of her art at **www.nancihersh.com.**

Proudly, ***Butterfly Kisses and Wishes on Wings*** has traveled to many parts of the world, and can be found in libraries, cancer centers, hospitals, and in the homes of many children and their families. For more information about our book, and additional resources on talking to kids about cancer, please log on to, ***www.butterflykissesbook.com***. You can also reach the author by phone at 303-589-2099.

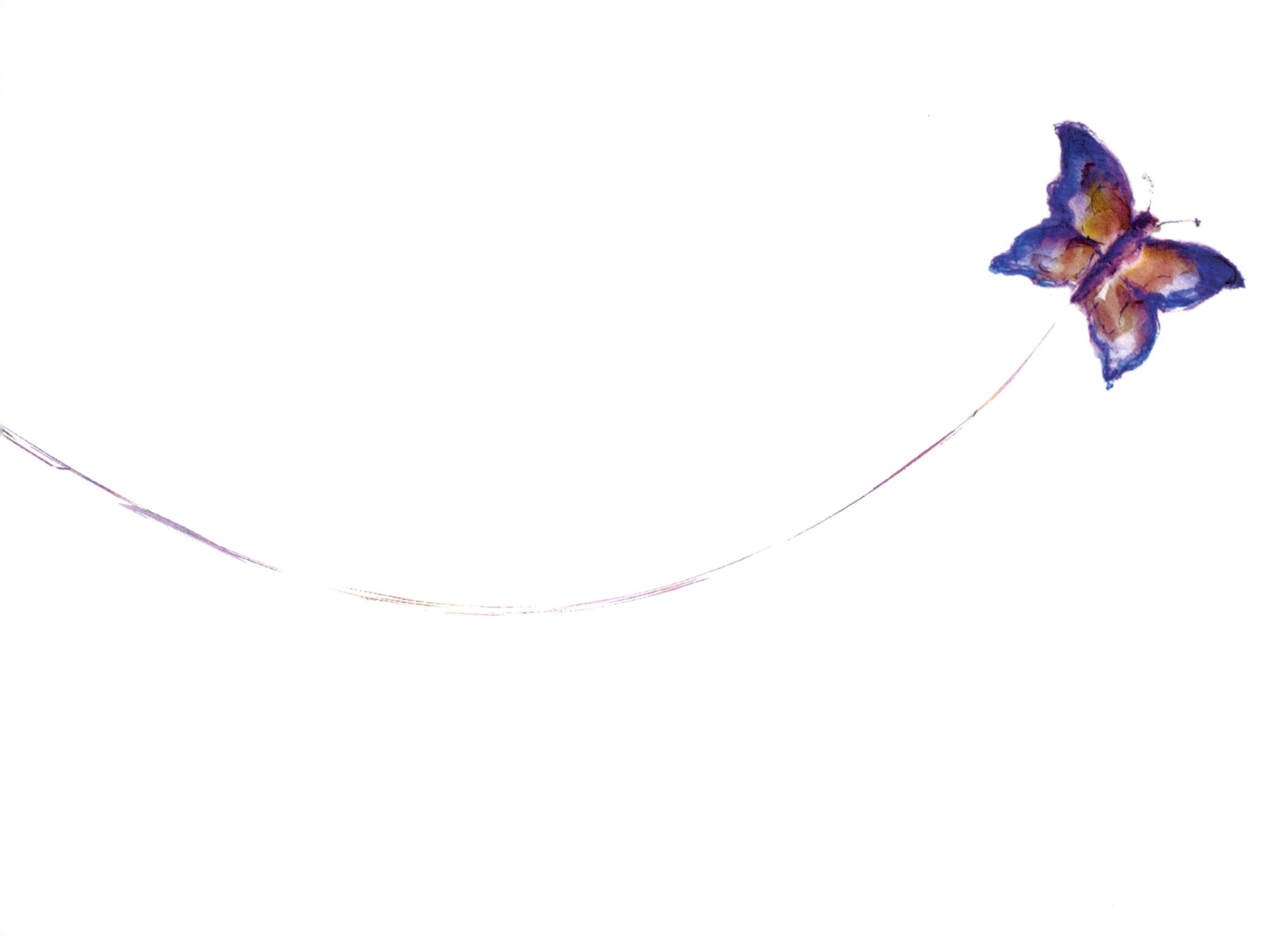